TIPS FROM

The

A GUIDE FOR MAKING A GREAT IMPRESSION ON CAMERA AND IN PERSON

D0927376

VALONDA CALLOWAY

TIPS FROM

The TV Lady®

Contents

Preface

Let's talk about my nickname, "The TV Lady." For as long as I have worked in front of the camera, people have called me, The TV Lady. I suppose some of it is because I live and work in the south, and we are traditionally proper, hence the word lady. The other part may be because my name is not common; therefore, some people cannot remember it or mispronounce it. I hear my nickname all the time. In the mall, at church, or social gatherings, someone is bound to yell out, "Hey, it's The TV Lady." It used to bother me, but not anymore. I embrace it. I am The TV Lady.

I have worked on-camera as either a news anchor and reporter, host, actor, or spokesperson for more than 20 years. You stop counting at 20, according to my colleague Melanie Sanders. I have learned a ton over the years, including what to wear, what not to wear, how to sit, how not to sit, how to position your body, and how not to. You get the idea. I have not worked a traditional job since 2016 when the Raleigh, NC based TV show I hosted, My Carolina Today/Talk, was canceled. Instead, I have worked as a freelancer, which gives me a lot of freedom and time.

So often, I find myself screaming at the TV or the computer when I see well-meaning people make mistakes with lighting, clothing, and makeup. It always leads my husband Randal, to smirk and say, "why don't you do something about it, TV lady?" He has been pushing me for years to take what I have learned and share it with the world. I got another nudge during the 2020 Coronavirus pandemic from my former boss, Kim Green. Kim had her own nickname for me when we worked together, "Upper Management." Even though my role was host, I took on a lot more responsibility than just being a host. I helped her book guests for the show, write the show's content, and manage and mentor interns. Sometimes Kim didn't have time to deal with certain things or didn't want to tell someone no and risk hurting their feelings. Her fallback would be, "I'll have to take that to upper management," or "unfortunately, upper management doesn't support that idea." We've had so many laughs over that nickname and the fact that I acted like a boss when I didn't have the title. Therefore, I wasn't surprised to get a text from her out of the blue, encouraging me to do a tutorial for black women wanting to do Facebook or YouTube videos. She also saw many mistakes when it came to lighting and sound. Kim's text stuck with me and I couldn't get it out of my head for weeks. I thought, yes, I'd love to help black women with lighting and sound, but these are issues that men and women of every skin tone need help with.

I finally decided to act when my dearest friends and Delta Sigma Theta Sorors Sharon Mosely and Shanta Jackson suggested I write this book. We get together regularly over a meal or over Zoom to talk about our entrepreneurial efforts. We encourage and hold each other accountable. Their push was the final one I needed to sit down and start typing. I guess I am like my daughter Lilyn who will not listen to a word I say but let a friend or another adult say the same thing, and it is the best thing she ever heard. Case in point, my husband, had been telling me in so many words to write the book. Sorry, Randal.

I have so many amazing people in my life whom I have learned from and collaborated with on this journey of showing off my best self. Sharon Delaney McCloud and I hosted My Carolina Today together. She is a powerhouse who left the show to start her own business. She brought me along to do many things, including media training. I cannot thank Sharon enough.

Let's travel down memory lane. I want to take you back to the '90s and my college experience. Debra Rivers Johnson was my cheerleading coach at Winston-Salem State University. Ms. Rivers understood that we could not just be great cheerleaders; we also had to look the part. She required our hair and makeup to be on point. After all, we represented our university, and she made sure we knew it and looked our best. Ms. Rivers is the reason I still wear red lipstick to this day. Revlon's Cherries In The Snow was her favorite!

After college, I landed my first job in Washington, DC, at The Voice Of America. Sidney Lippman was my editor. She taught me how to be a great writer and how to make it plain for an audience. By her example, she also taught me elegance and sophistication. I used to watch Sidney like a hawk. Her personality was super type-A, and I absolutely loved it. She took no bull, but she was graceful and elegant. When Randal and I got married, Sidney sent champagne flutes from

Tiffany. When I unwrapped the signature blue box, I thought to myself, "of course, Sidney would send me a gift from Tiffany. Where else would a classy woman like Sidney shop?" Those flutes are the only items from Tiffany I own.

When I became a TV reporter and anchor in Raleigh, NC, I met Monica Laliberte. We worked together at WRAL TV. She's a reporter and anchor too, but for a short stint, Monica was an Executive-Producer. She stayed on my ass about EVERYTHING. I will never forget the day she looked at my red hair and asked, "what is this?" She told me I needed to get the color fixed immediately. At that moment, I was so mad, but she was right. I learned so much from her. Thank you, Monica.

My first teacher was my mother, Sonzia Bruinton, a proper southern lady. She made sure I had shapewear even though I never weighed over 105 pounds as a teenager and a young lady. I sort of got it then, but I really get it now. It does not matter what size you are; all women need proper undergarments. More on that later. Thanks, Mom!

You know the saying; you don't know what you don't

know? It is true. I didn't know how bad my under-eye circles were until a professional makeup artist pointed it out to me when she came to a television station where I worked. After our conversation, I looked back at recordings of myself, and the darkness under my eyes was so clear, but I didn't see it. I am so thankful I listened to her and revamped my makeup. What matters most is that we learn and move on to bigger and better in terms of how we communicate and make a presence in the online world or in person. I am still working on a lot of these lessons myself. Yes, I still get checked from people who love me when I screw-up some of these finer points. So, do not beat yourself up if you have made some of the same mistakes I point out.

The bottom line is that people make judgements about us when they are watching us. It does not matter how many degrees you have or how long you have been doing what it is you do. If your presentation is shotty, people will discredit the information you are sharing. Many times, it is not even something we realize we are doing. Many super-smart people have studied this. Dr. Nick Morgan of Public Words Inc. found that our eyes take in 82 percent of the world around us and our ears only take in 11 percent. That explains a lot about why the visuals we create have to be just as strong, if not stronger, than the words we speak.

So here it is! This book is for anyone who wants to improve their presentation, whether on TV, YouTube, Facebook, Zoom, or in person. You will learn my persnickety ways when it comes to equipment like lighting, clothing, how you speak, and more. Distance working and learning are likely here to stay. Job interviews via digital platforms are the norm. The same first impression judgments that employers make in person are amplified even more online. A survey from Career Builder found that about 50 percent of employers knew within five minutes if an employee was a good fit for the position. It behooves all of us to get better at how to perform in this way. While pajamas might have been okay for some during the first week of Coronavirus stay at home orders, they will not fly anymore. By now, we should have it figured out.

I am here to help you figure it out. Tips From The TV Lady dives into why I make the suggestions I do. I give you examples and photos to show you what I mean, as well as advice from friends who are experts. Each chapter concludes with three memorable takeaways that will stick with you and that you can easily refer back to before you hit the start button on your next jewelry sale, job interview, or TV talk-back. When you're finished with Tips From The TV Lady, you will be ready to make a bigger and better impression and headed in the right direction to hit the intended mark. I'm rooting for you, now let's get to it!

Chapter One

DON'T WEAR THAT

Man, do I love animal print! When Randal and I started dating, he constantly poked fun at me over my love of animal print. I had the décor all over my condo, and I had plenty of clothing and shoes with the print as well. But that is not all. I thought I needed to have almost everything in the same color family, which meant I wore a lot of brown, tan, and... tan and brown. Bubblin' Brown Sugar, that was me. Check out our engagement photo. I am wearing a brown outfit and brown lipstick.

It was not until much later that I learned brown is one of the worst colors for me to wear on camera or for presenting. My skin is brown; therefore, a contrasting color works much better for me. I looked lost in a sea of brown. It is a good idea to work with a professional stylist who can show you the best colors for your skin tone. But until then, the primary and secondary colors work well for most people. My friend Sharon Delaney McCloud teaches media training to business executives. The topic of what to wear always strikes a chord. "Wear jewel tones. Despite what you may think, it is good to wear bright colors. Jewel tones are vibrant blues, green, red, purple, and orange," says Sharon.

Photo by Elizabeth Ashley & Co

Don't you dare wear a blah color like brown, grey, or taupe when presenting. Sharon says those colors won't draw the audience's eyes to you. "Muted colors like taupe and grey are not good choices when on camera, on a virtual conference or on stage. They tend to pull the color from your face, no matter what your complexion is. In addition, black and white can look dull on camera, especially in this age of HDTV, where colors practically jump off the screen." According to Sharon, the exception would be wearing a bright-colored blouse or dress shirt inside a dark or neutral blazer.

Photo by Joe Bradley

Now, let's talk about patterns. Just don't. But if you must, go with patterns that are not too busy or put the pattern on the bottom half of your outfit. Solids are a much better choice when you are presenting, whether on camera or in person.

Patterns can be too busy and sometimes they lead the eye to places you do not intend. On camera, some patterns can also lead to what is called a moiré effect. This is when you get the sensation that your eye is jumping because you see odd stripes and patterns. This problem happens mostly with tight patterns that you often find in men's shirts and ties. Men can avoid this by going with solids or patterns that are wide, not tight.

Look at my fine-ass husband! I took this photo of him at a wedding in 2018.

Here, he is a good example of how Sharon says men should dress when they are on camera. "There is a long-standing debate about whether men should wear white shirts; light blue is worn just as often. If you watch the Sunday-morning talk shows, you'll see that almost every male interviewed wears a navy-blue suit, white or light blue shirt, and a colorful tie. Navy is always a winner," says Sharon.

You want to look open and inviting when you speak to people, not closed off or as if you are hiding something. Because of this, avoid heavy scarfs around the neck and turtlenecks. If you are cold-natured like me, find another way to stay warm that does not involve closing off your neck.

I got the color right, but the scarf was all wrong.

Sharon says there's another reason to reveal your

neck, the slimming effect. "It makes you look thinner and elongates your torso. The rumors are true—TV adds about ten pounds. If you wear a turtleneck or high collar, it makes your neck disappear and tends to make you look wider."

When it comes to constructing your outfit, choose clothing that is simple and easy to wear. I once watched, or tried to watch, a Facebook video featuring a woman wearing a cowl neck sweater. She could not figure out how she wanted that neckline to lay. She tussled with it for the first two minutes of the video as she waited for people to join. Guess what? I left the live. It drove me crazy to watch her fuss with that sweater. After watching her do that, I no longer cared what she had to say.

Fashion stylist, April Clark, knows a thing or two about presenting well on camera. She has been a stylist for 11 years and was a style contributor to New York Live on NBC4 and My Carolina Today. April was also a personal stylist for Crabtree Valley Mall in Raleigh, NC. She says you should always try on your clothes before pressing the start button. "After you set up your camera, do a test run, and review it. Pay attention to the way your clothes are falling on your body. Make sure that you are wearing items that are comfortable while sitting down for an extended period. Fidgeting with your clothing while live is a no-no, even if it's just Facebook."

Accessories can also be a no-no. I once produced a TV show on a local NBC affiliate for a hip-hop music mogul. One of the show's guests arrived wearing a big gold chain with a big gold charm. I knew it would be a problem the moment he walked in the door. He sat down in his chair and a member of the floor crew put on his microphone. He immediately started fidgeting in his chair. Of course, the chain hit the mic, and it sounded terrible. I asked him to remove the chain. I knew what the answer would be, but I asked anyway. He said no. I explained to him that this chain was hitting the mic. It sounded terrible; therefore, his audio quality would suffer. Since he refused to remove the chain, I asked him to please try not to move too much or fidget. He said okay. As soon as the interview began, he moved in his chair and fidgeted. The audio was a mess.

Necklaces are not the only problem, according to stylist April Clark. "Instead of wearing two or three bracelets, limit yourself to one. The same goes for earrings. Wear a pair of earrings that do not make a lot of sound or make a lot of movement." April also cautions against high shine jewelry because it will be distracting under bright lights.

Have you seen the people who unknowingly reveal they are not wearing pants? You do not want to be in that club. April says you should get completely dressed. "In the era of Zoom meetings and live social TV, you're always on, and you never know when you'll have to move quickly. If the camera drops, you don't want it to reveal that you're not wearing any pants." April also says the act of getting dressed is psychological. "Getting completely dressed also makes you feel as if you are giving a real broadcast. Treat your live feeds as if you are on a major network. Show up, ready to go."

DON'T WEAR THAT
TV *Lady* TAKEAWAYS

1. WEAR PRIMARY OR SECONDARY COLORS

2. KEEP THE JEWELRY SIMPLE

3. GET COMPLETELY DRESSED

Chapter Two

GIRL, WHAT'S UNDER THAT SKIRT?

There is nothing wrong with stomach rolls, cellulite, and the like. A lot of us have it. I got a lot more of it after my pregnancy. I am proud of my body and I am thankful that I was fortunate enough to carry and deliver a human. But when I am all dressed up and before a crowd, I do not want the attention on my rolls. I want it on the message I am working to get across.

Shapewear is the difference between having a smooth and polished look and not. Let me be clear. This is not about size. It does not matter whether you are a size two or 22; shapewear can give you a put-together look. That is what you are going for when you are standing or sitting in front of people.

I will never forget shopping with my mother for my senior prom attire. Back then, I was around 95 pounds and a size zero. We bought a straight, floor-length, blue sequined gown. This dress fit me like a glove. There was no room for error. My mom knew that I had a good appetite and would go all out on dinner before the prom. My little belly would swell up like a balloon after a meal. In regular clothes, you could not tell. But in that straight, perfectly tailored gown, you would see it plain as day. That is why mom insisted on me wearing control top panties that would slim down my swollen belly and keep me from looking like I was five months pregnant at my senior prom. I did not get it at the time, but boy, am I glad she did.

Mom bought the panties at Sears. They were the ugliest, most old-school looking contraption I had ever seen. But they worked! I wore those panties under that dress and achieved the look mom and I were going for. The power of those panties made such an impression on me that I kept them and wore them any time I needed to put on a slim fitting special occasion dress. And guess what? I still have them, and I still wear them all these decades later. Sure, I could buy new ones, but I do not see any reason to. They worked then, and they work now. Plus, I see them as a tribute to my mother. Every time I wear them, I think of her, and I laugh out loud when I think about how right she was about them.

Photo by Roman Council

If you need to shop for shapewear, it is easy to find. You have probably heard of Spanx. You can find the brand in department stores and online. I have heard other people swear by them. Kim Kardashian West also has a line called Skims that is extremely popular. These two brands are on the pricier side. Believe it or not, Sears still sells shapewear. You may have trouble finding a physical store, but as of this writing, their online business is going strong, and their shapewear does not cost a whole lot.

Shapewear can smooth out all the places that might need it, including the breasts, stomach, hips, and thighs. Men are getting into it too. Offerings include tees and tanks. The products for men may be called shapewear, but you can also find them under compression clothing for men.

Shapewear is also essential when wearing clothing that is thin. You may not notice how thin your clothing is under the lights in your bedroom or bathroom. But you will certainly notice under professional lighting or even consumer lighting that you may buy for your virtual presentations.

GIRL, WHAT'S UNDER THAT SKIRT?
TV *Lady* TAKEAWAYS

1. SHAPEWEAR IS NOT ABOUT DRESS SIZE

2. LISTEN TO YOUR MOTHER

3. MEN WEAR SHAPEWEAR TOO

Chapter Three

EVERYBODY NEEDS MAKEUP

Makeup is designed to enhance your beauty and cover up your flaws. That is what I am asking you to do. I am not suggesting you turn into someone your friends and family members would not recognize. Makeup allows you to cut down on distractions that may come when audiences drift. People will notice if your forehead is oily, dark circles under your eyes, and if your lips are chapped. Remember, you want them listening to what you have to say, not picking apart your face.

If you are not a makeup aficionado, do not worry. Heavy makeup is not necessary. Invest in just a few items; concealer under the eyes, a pop of color on the lips, powder to reduce the shine, or blotting sheets to soak up the oil. I'm a big fan of blotting sheets and I have my own line of them.

Men need to at least wear powder or use blotting sheets, especially bald men. To use a blotting sheet, press the sheet onto the oily parts of your face, hold it there for a second or two, and then remove. The sheet will absorb the oil from your skin.

If you have no idea where to go, the makeup counter at a department store in the mall or a beauty store is a good place to start. The men and women at these counters can match you with the best powder for your skin tone. I love the makeup at the drug stores but going there is only a good idea if you know what you are looking for.

I went to a beauty expert to get her take on wearing makeup. Sharon Davis, of Sharon S. Davis Makeup Artistry, is a friend of mine and a 15-year veteran of the industry. "For an office look or business look, you need to be polished and wear matte makeup. You shouldn't have a shiny, shimmery, or glowy look." Sharon suggests matte for the foundation, eye shadow, and blush. "You want to be taken seriously, and for the people you're talking to, to understand who you are," says Sharon.

Sharon has great makeup advice for men too. I was pleasantly surprised to hear that men are going even further than I knew. "I have several male clients who are more comfortable now than they've ever been. Most men now are used to being pampered." Sharon says her male clients are not shy about expressing what they need. "They'll say, wake me up, I look tired."

Sharon has some tried and true tricks for her male clients. "A little concealer is the quickest fix for the tiredness and under-eye shadow. Powder helps, and we don't want the eyebrow hair everywhere." Sharon says men should brush their eyebrow hair up. Guys, if you really want to step-up your game, take this advice from Sharon. "Tinted moisturizer hydrates the skin and adds a little color, and I've even put dark brown or clear mascara on men to open their eyes up." Sharon shared two photos of clients she's worked with to cover problem areas and achieve a polished professional look.

Problem areas: Dry skin, hair growth, which cast a shadow in the jaw area, and hypopigmentation in the cheek area

Problem areas: Dry skin, redness in the cheek area, and under-eye area; and hair growth that cast a shadow in the jaw area

Both men had skin issues that she corrected with makeup. Sharon applied a pea-size amount of concealer under the eyes and concealer on top of the five o'clock shadow. She mixed foundation into a moisturizer and applied it to their foreheads, cheeks, chins, and above the lips. She also tapped powder into their T-zone areas and cheeks. Finally, Sharon brushed their eyebrows upward, applied clear mascara and lip moisturizer, blotted with a tissue to remove the excess shine.

If you are a makeup aficionado, be careful not to go overboard. How much makeup you wear really depends on your topic and your audience. I did a commercial for Aflac, the insurance company, where I played a novice online workout instructor. The instructions from the production company were for me to wear very natural makeup. Lashes and red lipstick were not necessary.

I am wearing plenty of makeup, but the colors and application is light. I am wearing foundation, concealer, blush, eyeliner, mascara, eye shadow in my eyebrows, and light pink lipstick.

In a video for IBM, I played a boss. Again, plenty of makeup but not glamour makeup.

I do wear glamour makeup from time to time. When I emceed a wedding industry fashion show, I had full-on glam, including lashes, bold lips, bold eyes, bold everything. Sharon Davis did my makeup and blew me away with her artistry.

Photo by Jeffrey Lynn Media Photography

If you can swing it, hire a professional makeup artist, and tell him or her the look you are going for. When you find the right artist, your face is one less thing to worry about as you prepare for your on-camera or in-person presentation.

Remember, in the preface, where I wrote that I still make mistakes and get checked by people who love me? This is one of those moments. I stood before my mirror, getting ready for a shoot one day when my daughter Lilyn, who was 12 at the time, checked me on my makeup. I was stunned as my YouTube makeup tutorial watching pre-teen put me in check. The conversation went like this.

Lilyn: "Mom, you need to bake."

Me: "Huh?"

Lilyn: "Bake your face!"

Me: "Lilyn, I don't know what that means."

Lilyn: "Your concealer is too light. You need to bake under your eyes."

Me: "Really?" (As I step back to look at my eyes.)

Lilyn: "Yeah."

Me: "Oh. You're right. How do I bake?"

Lilyn: "I'll be right back."

Me: Waiting.

Lilyn: "Here, use this powder from my palette."

Me: I do it.

Lilyn: "You need a smaller brush. Here use this."

Me: I do it some more, "Is this better?"

Lilyn: "Yeah, mom, that looks good."

Me: "Thanks!"

Lilyn: "Oh, you looked like that yesterday too."

Lilyn doing my makeup at age 10.

The finished product.

EVERYBODY NEEDS MAKEUP
TV *Lady* TAKEAWAYS

1. WEAR MATTE MAKEUP FOR A
PROFESSIONAL LOOK

2. MEN SHOULD WEAR CONCEALER AND
GROOM THEIR BROWS

3. CHILDREN WILL LEAD THE WAY

Chapter Four

GOT A LIGHT?

If you are making a video or doing a live on social media, you will almost always need to add artificial lighting. Because of social media, lights are now an affordable consumer product. You could go as basic as a ring light to a more complex dimmable light for cameras with filters. For suggestions, I consulted my friend, photojournalist Pete James. Pete is the proud recipient of an Edward R. Murrow Award, and he has been nominated for an Emmy Award five times. Pete says you probably already have a light source at home to use. "A lot of people may not have professional lights, but most people have access to some type of lamp. If you have a lamp, take your lamp shade off, sit close to that light, and it will be enough to make your face visible."

If you would like to go a step further and buy professional lighting, Pete says you can start with just one. "That light should have a direct path to your face, and you should set it up higher." You can use a tape measure to get the right height, but Pete says there is always a workaround. "If you sit down in your chair, just raise your arm in the air, and then set the light to that height." Pete says a light about a foot above your head, shining down toward your face, is the optimal position.

Lighting is not something to rush into. You will need to test out your lighting to ensure you do not cause shadows or make yourself look overexposed. You can do that by adjusting the height of the lights, the distance from you, as well as the brightness. Trust me; you will be much happier with how you look when the lighting is right.

Photo by Elizabeth Ashley & Co

If you are interviewing someone or including an-other person in your video who is of a different skin tone than you are, be sure to adjust the light. A dark-skinned Black person will need different lighting than a fair-skinned White person. In this example, if you give both people the same light, one person may look washed out while the other may look too dark.

Nothing beats mother nature when it comes to light. Sunlight, or ambient light, is often the only thing you need, but you must use it wisely. The sun should be on your face, not behind you. If you make a video or do a live with your back to a window or outside with your back to the sun, you will be backlit, or in other words, dark; unless you compensate with artificial light. Professional photographers and videographers know how to navigate this, but the average person should just turn around and make use of the light.

Getting the light on your face does not always feel good. When I was a novice news reporter, I would often do live reports on location. Sometimes the sun was not where we needed it to be to show the TV audience the scene and, at the same time, have me looking my best. To compensate, photographers would use a gigantic reflector to bounce the light onto my face. Boy, would I complain about it because the light would be so intense that I would have to squint to keep my eyes open. It often made my eyes water. Despite my complaining, most of the time, the photographers did not relent. With hindsight being 20/20, I am glad they did not listen to me. They knew what they were doing.

There is a funny story behind the next picture. I was getting ready to emcee a wedding reception and walked across the mostly empty room before guests had arrived. The wedding photographer, Keith Cephus, yelled to me to stop! I did not know what was going on. He then told me that the light coming through the window was perfect, and he wanted to snap my picture. Boy, was he right. I absolutely love this photo. My face was perfectly positioned in the ambient light.

Photo by Keith Cephus

GOT A LIGHT?
TV *Lady* TAKEAWAYS

1. USE A LAMP WITHOUT THE LAMP
   SHADE IF NECESSARY

2. SET ARTIFICIAL LIGHT AN ARM'S LENGTH
   ABOVE YOUR HEAD

3. TURN YOUR FACE TOWARDS THE SUN

Chapter Five

LET'S TALK ABOUT SETS

Admit it. You do it. What, you ask? Look in the background of people's photos, videos, and social media live videos to see what is going on. I suppose it is human nature and nosiness. Since we know this will happen, put some thought into your background or set before you get started. You want to make sure your set is a clutter-free, embarrassment-free zone. As a reminder, you want the focus on the message you are sharing, not on the background.

Go for depth! Do not shove your chair against the wall. You should be separated from the background. When you put your chair against the wall, you can cause shadows on the wall if you are using a light, and you should be using a light. Instead, set up in an area that allows for space behind you. That space should be lovely. Perhaps a room with a pretty picture on the wall, or a nice bookcase. If you do not have such a space, look around for a blank wall or a wall with minimal distractions. Put a plant, flowers, or small piece of décor in that space.

A lovely living room, isn't it? It doesn't belong to anyone I know. I downloaded it from Shutterstock. You can do the same. Shutterstock is one of many websites that sells beautiful virtual backgrounds.

If you do not have a suitable space in your home or office, a backdrop may be just what you need. Backdrops come in many different colors. Grey is one of the best choices because it is easier to light than black or white. Typically, the backdrop is foldable and comes with an adjustable stand and clips to attach the fabric. You can easily buy one online, and it is not cost-prohibitive. If you plan to be live or make videos often, a backdrop is the way to go. You can fold it away when you are not using it. But of course, you do not have to buy one. You may have what you need in your linen closet. Look for a grey bed sheet or blanket. Test it out on your wall and see if it works.

Screenshot from an audition I recorded at a studio using a grey backdrop.

How you position your computer, tablet, or phone is key. Your device should be eye level. If it is lower than eye level, that means the audience is looking up your nose. That does not look good on anybody. Photojournalist Pete James says it also creates another problem for your overall look. "When you are looking down, you create a double chin effect, and that is not flattering. You almost want to look up. You do not want the praying to Jesus look up, but just have a slight tilt to your head. That way, you eliminate any type of double chin action." No matter the device, use an adjustable stand or stack it up on books or whatever you can find to lift your device to eye level.

Be careful about your headroom. Headroom is the space above your head. I have seen far too many ceiling tiles during interviews on TV and social media. This mistake happens when the laptop is tilted too far back. A better choice is to adjust your chair and slide the computer forward or backward. You only need about an inch, maybe an inch and a half, of space above your head. It is important to have that little bit of extra space because most of us naturally move our bodies when we talk. If you have less than an inch, you could cut off your head if you start moving around as you are talking.

My former boss, Kim Green, worked as a producer in TV news and lifestyle TV for more than 20 years. She is now a corporate video producer for a Fortune 100 company. Kim says she has noticed a recurring problem. "Since the majority of my work is now virtual, I am on a lot of video calls. One of the issues I have seen is the glasses glare. The glare is caused by the reflection of a computer monitor in the lenses of the glasses. It keeps viewers from seeing your eyes, and it is distracting." Kim suggests taking off your glasses or turning down the brightness on your monitor.

A lot of us have ticks or nervous energy things we do that we do not notice but are noticeable to everyone else. I once sat through a Zoom call with six people and one of them clicked his pen the entire time. It was so annoying, but he was the boss, and I was a guest, not an employee of his company. I did not feel it was my place to tell him to stop. Another annoying thing that sometimes happens is leaning on the desk, something Kim has had to deal with. "During a recording with a presenter over video chat, we noticed the camera kept shaking. It turned out the presenter was leaning on his desk, causing the camera to shake. We stopped recording and had the presenter stand up to stop the problem." Kim says that while it seemed like a minor shake on the presenter's end, it was a bouncing screen for the viewers.

Unless your video or live is quick, please do not hold your device in your hand. After more than two minutes, your arm will get tired, and the video will be shaky. It is best to put a phone or tablet on a stand. If you use a phone, make sure to turn it horizontally, not vertically. The horizontal position fills the screen. If your phone is vertical, the viewer will see blank space to the left and the right of your video or live shot.

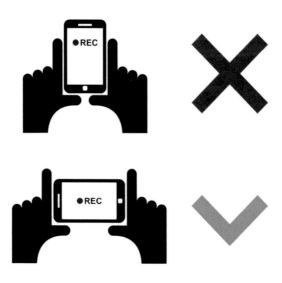

Perhaps you have an old computer that does not have an internal webcam, or your computer has a webcam, but the resolution on the cam is bad. Unfortunately, that is the case on a lot of laptops. If you think your webcam might not be ready for prime-time, test it out. A bad webcam will show you looking dark or grainy. It may even have a pixelated look. Do not worry. You can buy a webcam and attach it to your computer. The webcam plugs into your USB port and attaches to the top of your monitor. Webcams are affordable. I have seen them priced from $10 to more than $200. Of course, you get what you pay for, so check out the specs and choose the best webcam based on how you plan to use it. I should also tell you that when the Covid-19 crisis hit the United States in 2020, it seemed everybody in the entire country wanted a webcam. They were extremely hard to find. If you plan to use a webcam, do not wait until the last minute to get one. They could be on backorder or you could be left without a variety of choices on which one to buy.

LET'S TALK ABOUT SETS
TV *Lady* TAKEAWAYS

1. PICK A PRETTY, EMBARRASSMENT-FREE BACKGROUND

2. A GREY BACKDROP IS EASIEST TO LIGHT

3. YOUR DEVICE SHOULD BE EYE LEVEL

Chapter Six

HEY, OVER HERE

It can be confusing to know exactly where to fix your gaze when talking to an online audience. I once saw a man being interviewed live on the news via Zoom, who seemed so distracted. His set looked nice, but it was clear that he was watching himself on TV as he conducted his interview. Instead of looking directly at his laptop camera, he kept looking up as he talked. My guess is that the TV in his home was mounted on the wall and he wanted to look there to check himself out. What he failed to realize was that his looking up was extremely distracting for the viewer.

If you are on a business video call or being interviewed, whether for the news, a job, or anything else, look at the camera. You especially want to look at the camera if it is for a job interview. Your gaze could affect your wallet. Remember, first impressions are super important. It can be difficult to look people in the eye if you do not practice it. With so many of us working remotely, we have gotten out of practice when it comes to looking at real human beings in person.

You have to work a bit harder to be engaging in a digital space versus in person. Looking directly into the camera lens is the equivalent of looking someone in the eye. Looking up at a TV hanging on the wall is the same as looking away from the person talking to you. Attaching a sticky note or a red dot right beside your camera to remind you to look into the lens is a great way to fix this issue. It is natural to look at the screen to address the person who is asking you a question or to listen to another person talking. But please remember, when it is your time to shine, give eye contact.

When it comes to eye contact in a digital space, it is important to think of the things you do when talking with someone in person. If you normally talk with your hands, don't stop just because you are communicating digitally. You will want to back away from the computer a bit so that your hands can be seen in the frame. You will also want to record yourself having a conversation with a friend or family member before having an important meeting or presentation. Do this to make sure your hands are communicating what you want them to.

HEY, OVER HERE
TV *Lady* TAKEAWAYS

1. LOOK AT THE WEBCAM FOR EYE CONTACT

2. USE A STICKY NOTE NEXT TO THE WEBCAM
TO REMIND YOURSELF TO LOOK THERE

3. TALK WITH YOUR HANDS IF THAT'S
WHAT YOU NORMALLY DO

Chapter Seven

CAN YOU HEAR ME NOW?

What is the point of doing a live shot or a Zoom or Skype call if the audience cannot clearly hear you? It is truly a waste of time. Have you seen the videos that buffer and prevent you from clearly seeing and hearing the person talking? During the 2020 presidential campaign, I heard a caller to a radio show make an important point about digital communication. He was critical of a candidate because of the way she sounded when she called in to this show. Her signal was shaky and that caused a lot of buffering and delays. The caller was left with the impression that the candidate did not care about the show's audience because she did not make sure she had a clear and strong signal. I am sure the candidate would be disappointed to hear that her call-in left some listening audience members with a sour taste.

There are a couple of things you can do to make sure that does not happen to you. Simply put, you need a strong internet connection or cell phone signal. If you can, position yourself near your internet router or connect your computer to the router via an ethernet cord. If that is not possible, get a signal booster to improve your cell signal. At times, I have had to ask everyone in the house to get off the internet while I was using it to get a strong signal.

Once you have a strong signal, whether by computer or phone, make sure your audio is good. Earbuds and wired headphones with a built-in microphone work well for Zoom, Skype, etc. Having a microphone close to your mouth cuts down on background noise that can interrupt your sound.

I prefer to use a microphone to make sure I am heard loud and clear. I have clip-on mics, also known as lavalier microphones, that I clip to my lapel or neckline. They plug into the USB port of my computer. If I am using my phone, I use an adapter so that I can plug in the microphone. If the mic has a cord, make sure the cord is under your shirt, not on top of it. The visible cord looks sloppy and is a distraction.

If you use a lavalier microphone, do not wear a necklace, and make sure your hair does not touch the microphone. When something like a necklace or hair rubs against the microphone, the audience can hear it. It is distracting and takes away from what you have to say. You may not even notice that it is happening, so it is best to avoid anything that could get in the way of optimal sound.

Another microphone option I have available is one that I primarily use to record voice-overs. It sits on a stand and is large. I have only used it once during a Zoom, and that was because my husband was joining me for the call, and I wanted both of us to be clearly heard.

Whatever you use to amplify your sound, test it out first. Whether you are using Zoom, Skype, Teams, etc., they all allow you to test your audio before you get started. Before you log on to any of these tools, you can also test the audio on your computer by going to settings.

One more thing: no matter how much we prepare, technology sometimes fails us. My daughter took dance classes over Zoom after the Coronavirus pandemic sent everyone home. On the first day of class, one of her teachers showed up about 25 minutes late. The students and parents were all worried about what was going on. It turned out, the cable company had an outage and the teacher was not able to get onto Zoom from her computer. She had to download the app to her phone to teach the class. This is why I suggest you have your preferred video conferencing platform on your computer and your phone or tablet.

CAN YOU HEAR ME NOW?
TV *Lady* TAKEAWAYS

1. GET A STRONG INTERNET CONNECTION

2. USE A MICROPHONE

3. TEST YOUR AUDIO IN ADVANCE

Chapter Eight

SITTING PRETTY

I was a pageant girl. I loved them. Any excuse to get on stage and dance was all I needed to hear. But I also enjoyed getting dressed up, wearing glamorous makeup, and making new friends. One thing I did not realize I would appreciate at the time, but I do now, is all the lessons I learned about poise. Most of those lessons came when I competed in the Onslow County Junior Miss program, a preliminary to North Carolina's Junior Miss and America's Junior Miss. The program is now called Distinguished Young Women. Junior Miss was different because it did not consider itself a pageant, but rather a scholarship program. We did not have a swimsuit competition, and grades carried a significant amount of weight. We spent many months together preparing for the competition. It felt like a family rather than a competition. There were sleepovers, pool parties, and poise sessions. Those poise sessions included how to be interviewed. We were taught how to sit in a chair, what to do with our hands and legs, and scan a panel of people with our eyes. I have used those lessons ever since. Thank you, Mr. Wall and your entire team!

I couldn't find my Junior Miss photos, but here's a photo from when I was Teen Miss Downeast.

If you plan to sit for your interview, presentation, or talk, do not be drawn to the most comfortable chair in your house. That is probably the worst chair to use. Instead, maybe think of the most uncomfortable chair in your house. Sounds backwards, doesn't it? Here's why. When we are comfortable, we tend to slouch and show overall bad posture. Big, cushy chairs with arms allow us to sink in and feel at home. Instead, it is better to sit in a firm chair without arms. Do not scoot your butt all the way to the back of the chair. This will allow you to sit up straight and keep good posture instead of leaning too far back and slumping.

When you are sharing electronically, a medium to close-up shot is most appropriate. If you need a wide shot for some reason, be sure to cross your legs at the ankle, if you must cross. Guys, please avoid manspreading. That is when you sit with your legs spread far apart, taking up more space than one person needs. If you were to manspread on a bus or subway, you would take up more than one seat.

Many people, especially women, consider manspreading rude. It sends the signal that a man wants to take up more space than is necessary and therefore encroach on others' rights. It can also draw your eye to the man's crotch. Unless you are doing a video for an adult outlet, or adult purposes, that is not where we want the viewer's attention to go. The manspreading problem is so bad that municipalities have launched public service campaigns about it around the world.

Here is a poster from a 2019 campaign in the Washington, DC subway system.

A better choice for men would be to sit with your legs apart in the 12–15 inches range. When a man sits this way, he is still comfortable, but not too comfortable.

If you wear a jacket, be sure to sit on the tail of the jacket. This will ensure your shoulders look smooth instead of having creases or a crumpled-up look. This advice goes for men and women. You should also un-button the lower button, sometimes the top one too, of the jacket for the same reason.

I should tell you how I did in the Onslow County Junior Miss program. Not too shabby if I do say so myself. I did not win, but I was the fourth runner-up (out of 15). I won the physical fitness award, and I was one of two winners in the evening gown category.

SITTING PRETTY
TV *Lady* TAKEAWAYS

1. PICK A CHAIR WITHOUT ARMS

2. SIT YOUR BUTT HALFWAY ON THE CHAIR

3. DON'T MANSPREAD

Chapter Nine

SHARING IS CARING

You've mastered delivering your message all by yourself and now you want to involve other people. Great! Take all the lessons I have shared with you and share them with your guest. It would be a shame for you to look amazing and your guest not to look his or her best. Of course, you cannot force this excellence on other people, but at least try to help the people you will include in your live or recorded video look as good as they possibly can.

When you share the scene with someone over a platform like Zoom or Skype, try to match up your angles. If you have one inch of headroom, so should your guest. If you have one inch of headroom and your guest has three, the look will be distracting.

In other words, if person A is taking up more space than person B, person B will not command the same amount of attention, and maybe even credibility. If you look smaller, the audience may perceive you as smaller. This is an easy fix. Simply ask your guest to move his or her chair closer or further from the computer. Tilting the computer monitor forward or backward can also help.

Sharing the scene on a social media platform like Instagram is a whole other can of worms. Because Instagram is designed for phones, some of my rules of engagement will not work. You can invite someone to join you in a live and the person on the bottom of the phone screen will have comments and reactions obstructing his or her video. There is not much you can do about that, except accept it. After the live has ended, it can be posted to Instagram stories. The comments and reactions will not show up in the story, and the person's face on the bottom will be free of obstructions.

If you make plans in advance of your Instagram live, you can give your viewers a better experience. One workaround is to encourage your followers to watch the Instagram live on their computer versus their phone. In my opinion, Instagram looks better on the computer. The comments and reactions show up on the right side of the video versus on top of the video.

Sharing to more than one platform at the same is a time saver and a way to reach many audiences at the same time. There are several platforms offering this service, including OBS (Open Broadcaster Software), Restream, and Wirecast, to name a few. Some of them are free and some require a subscription. Streamyard is a popular streaming service that offers free and paid subscriptions. It is often used to interview guests, share screens, and more. It also allows streaming directly to most social media platforms to include Facebook, Youtube, and LinkedIn. Which platform you choose depends on whether you plan to broadcast casually or on a regular basis.

SHARING IS CARING
TV *Lady* TAKEAWAYS

1. MAKE SURE YOUR ANGLES MATCH

2. KNOW YOUR PLATFORMS

3. CONSIDER SHARING TO SEVERAL
PLATFORMS AT ONCE

Chapter Ten

WHO ARE YOU?

Big successful brands know exactly who they are, and we immediately recognize them. Target has their bullseye and Chick-fil-A has their cows. You should brand yourself as well. In some instances, you have to work a little harder to come across as your genuine self when reaching people virtually. You cannot communicate through a Zoom box all the things you can communicate when sitting or standing across from someone in person. Virtual communication does give you a bigger audience and more opportunities to reach people than ever before. The drawback, though, because everybody is doing it, the landscape is more crowded. Branding yourself is a way to stand out. After all, there is only one, you.

Derrick and me

Derrick Phillips is a business coach and branding expert. He is also one of the sharpest dressers I have ever
met in my life. Derrick says your brand is all about the
energy you put into the atmosphere. "Your brand is

not just your logo or design, but it's what people know, like, and trust about you." Derrick says this is known as the KLT Factor. It is a great place to start when you think about who you are to an audience. "The KLT factor is so important. We trust Walmart because we know we are going to get low prices. We trust Target because we know we are going to get something chic. What do you want people to know about you?"

Of course, the opposite of knowing, liking, and trusting someone is not knowing them, hating them, and having a lack of trust. If there is a negative connotation associated with you and your brand, Derrick says you cannot brush that under the rug. "You can't rebrand bad behavior or character. There are foundational things you have to clean up. If you are known for being reckless or scamming people, people will correlate that with your brand. The CEO can often time bring a bad name to a brand because of something they've done. When we develop a brand, we have to think in multiple layers." It can sometimes take an entire PR department working overtime to get past a crisis. Many solopreneurs and small businesses don't have that. That's why it is so important to think about what we're showing the world, whether we're on the clock or not.

While colors and logos are not the first ideas to consider when determining your brand, they are critically important. Derrick says we should all give these ideas serious consideration. "Certain colors will evoke certain emotions. For example, blue evokes trust and pink evokes calm."

According to Derrick, these are questions to ask yourself. What are you trying to communicate with your brand, where are you coming from, and where are you going?

Derrick says any time you are on camera; you are a billboard for your brand. "Incorporate your brand colors into what you present on camera. Any time I'm on camera, you'll see blue. Position yourself in the best light, so people get the same thing every time."

It is important to have some direction when you go live. The days of waiting for people to join and rambling for five minutes before you get to the point are over. Remember, some people in your audience will watch the replay instead of catching your broadcast live. You don't want people on the replay to have to fast forward to find the point where you begin sharing your message. Just like radio hosts, you can recap why you're live throughout your broadcast. "Map out your content strategy when sharing online. Think about, am I sharing too much? There is a thin line between too much and not enough," says Derrick.

Not sure who you are? Hire a brand strategist like Derrick. But you can get started by asking yourself what you think about all the time and lean into that. I'll use my sister Michelle as an example. Her day job is healthcare sales, but she loves interior design and making improvements to her home, and anybody else's home who will let her. She is so into home décor' that she is on a first-name basis with the managers at Lowe's Home Improvement. Michelle's real estate agent suggested she become a home stager or a real estate agent. She's now working on both. Her design aesthetic matches up perfectly with who she is. Michelle likes to look pretty and she likes pretty things around her. When you walk into her home, there's no question who lives there. The house looks like her.

The bottom line is that your brand should be about your authentic self. When you get it right, it won't feel forced. For years I thought about writing a book. I contributed a chapter to a book a few years ago, but I didn't actually write one on my own until a topic that was authentic to me reared its beautiful head. Helping people present their best selves on camera and in person is what I do. Therefore, writing Tips From The TV Lady came easy. Choosing my brand colors was a no-brainer. I learned years ago that cobalt blue was one of the best colors to wear on TV. I wear it all the time. Industry folks call it TV blue. When I researched the color, I found that it lined up with what I wanted to get across; trust, reliability, order. The only element I had to put some thought into was a companion color. I landed on coral. I love the color, and it symbolizes light and life.

Take a moment and ask yourself, "who are you?" Ask your friends and family the same question. If you are living in authenticity, the answers will line up and you'll know the direction to head in to make the most of your business, job, or whatever you're working on at the time.

WHO ARE YOU?
TV *Lady* TAKEAWAYS

1. KNOW YOUR KLT FACTOR

2. CHOOSE BRAND COLORS CAREFULLY

3. YOU ARE A BILLBOARD FOR YOUR BRAND

Thank you for reading Tips From The TV Lady. It was a tremendous joy to write. The words poured out of me because this is what I eat, sleep, and breathe. It was a hoot to poke fun at myself, especially about that engagement picture. It was great to reminisce with my parents as we talked about my pageant days while looking for pageant photos.

Getting to a place where I could offer advice has been a journey. I certainly didn't get here alone. I especially enjoyed writing about the people I admire and who have helped me get to where I am. I believe in giving people their flowers while they are here on earth to smell them, not at a funeral.

Now that you know my tips, please put them into practice one at a time. I don't want you to be overwhelmed. Sometimes when I get overwhelmed, I feel stuck and do nothing, rather than a little something. I would hate for that to happen to you. The end of the book has all the tips, broken into chapters, in one place. I did that so that you could quickly check the tips as you prepare for your next on-camera or in-person presentation.

I can't wait to see your transformations. Tag me on social media so that I can give you an atta-boy or atta-girl. You can find my handles on the last page. Go be great gorgeous!

TV *Lady* TAKEAWAYS

CHAPTER ONE
DON'T WEAR THAT

Wear Primary or Secondary Colors
Keep The Jewelry Simple
Get Completely Dressed

CHAPTER TWO
GIRL, WHAT'S UNDER THAT SKIRT?

Shapewear Is Not About Dress Size
Men Wear Shapewear Too
Listen To Your Mother

CHAPTER THREE
EVERYBODY NEEDS MAKEUP

Wear Matte Makeup For A Professional Look
Men Should Wear Concealer and Groom Their
Brows
Children Will Lead The Way

CHAPTER FOUR
GOT A LIGHT?

Use A Lamp Without The Lamp Shade If Necessary
Set Artificial Light An Arm's Length Above Your
Head
Turn Your Face Towards The Sun

CHAPTER FIVE
LET'S TALK ABOUT SETS

Pick A Pretty, Embarrassment-Free Background
A Grey Backdrop Is Easiest To Light
Your Device Should Be Eye Level

CHAPTER SIX
HEY, OVER HERE

Look At The Webcam For Eye Contact
Use A Sticky Note Next To The Webcam To
Remind Yourself To Look There
Talk With Your Hands If That's What You Normally
Do

CHAPTER SEVEN
CAN YOU HEAR ME NOW?

Get A Strong Internet Connection
Use A Microphone
Test Your Audio In Advance

CHAPTER EIGHT
SITTING PRETTY

Pick A Chair Without Arms
Sit Your Butt Halfway On The Chair
Don't Manspread

CHAPTER NINE
SHARING IS CARING

Make Sure Your Angles Match
Know Your Platforms
Consider Sharing To Several Platforms At Once

CHAPTER TEN
WHO ARE YOU?

Know Your KLT Factor
Choose Brand Colors Carefully
You Are A Billboard For Your Brand

Acknowledgments

Whew! 2020 has been something else, hasn't it? For me, it led to a lot of reflection and appreciation. If not for the way things shook out this year, this book may not have happened.

I'd like to first acknowledge my ancestors on both the Bruinton side and the Thomas side for the DNA they passed down. I have strength, courage, and wisdom because of them, and I lean on those qualities to get through challenges. I come from a big family, and I have always cherished my family ties, but I appreciate them now more than ever. I want to pay special tribute to the women.

I am Valonda,
a daughter of Sonzia,
who was a daughter of Charity,
who was a daughter of Lydia.

As my ancestors would say, I want to give honor to God, who is the head of my life. Sometimes my talks with God last a long time and sometimes they are only a few minutes. But the first thing I say every morning before my feet hit the floor is, "thank you, Jesus." The simple act of waking up is something to be thankful for and I'm so glad God isn't through with me yet.

Thank you, Randal, for pushing me to share all of this. For years you have nudged me to do it and I'm so grateful you didn't give up. I have a lot of ideas and it can be hard to keep up with what I've got going on at any given time. Thank you for being a supportive, loving husband.

Thank you, Lilyn, for being such a bright light. You are smart and witty, and you keep me laughing all the time. You also gave me great content for this book! I am so proud to be your mom.

Thank you, mom, dad, Michelle, Andre', Jacinta, and Chase. Your love and support mean the world to me. Thank you for putting up with my bossiness and loving me anyway. Thank you, Uncle Vic, for being so thoughtful in making sure I always have plenty of food and beautiful flowers and plants.

I have the world's greatest in-laws! Thank you, Richard and Sylvia Calloway, for being awesome cheerleaders and always sharing an encouraging word.

I have several girlfriends who have encouraged me and shared ideas while this book was still in my head and once I started the process. Sharon Mosely and Shanta Jackson, our Zoom meetings, are priceless. Thank you for always having a bright idea and for holding me accountable. Delani Mann, I treasure our Lake Lynn walk and talks and our patio pontifications. Lecha Watkins, Rhonda Harrison, and Dee Dee Burgess thank you for listening to my ideas and being so supportive of yet another one. Thank you, Kim Green, Alison Blevins, and Sharon Delaney McCloud, my work friends who became a lot more. Your encouraging words and actions mean more than you know.

I have several friends in real life whom I can always count on to share quotes and musings in person, on the phone, or social media, letting me know I'm on the right track. Thank you, Nicki Bradberry, Robert Hartwell, Derrick Phillips, Yolanda Rabun, and Kirstie Spadie. You all have the kind of energy the world needs more of.

This book could not have come together without the help of a fabulous team. Thank you to my literary midwife Angela Anderson for your editing and guidance. Your beautiful spirit also made this journey a joyful one. Thank you Stacey Blake for the fantastic formatting. You are so responsive and professional. Thank you, Rebecca Pau, for the awesome cover design. Ashley Green, you outdid yourself with the photos. I love them. Thank you! Thank you, Sharon Davis, for the outstanding job on my makeup and for your quotes inside the book. Thank you to my colorist Colesha Hagans for making sure my hair color was on point. Tyra Dixon, we have seen some stuff, haven't we? Thank you for your work behind the lens to promote this book. April Clark, you sparked so many amazing ideas. What a role model you are! Thank you for sharing your knowledge. Thank you, Nikki Davis, for pointing me in the right direction as I worked to put this book together.

I was going to skip the acknowledgments because I feared I would forget to acknowledge someone important and hurt feelings. My literary midwife Angela and my sister Michelle insisted that I had to do it. I'm sorry to anyone I should have listed here but didn't. Please charge it to my head and not my heart.

Valonda

About the Author

Valonda Calloway is a native of Richlands, in eastern North Carolina. She graduated cum laude from Winston-Salem State University. She began her career in media as a writer and reporter at the Voice of America radio in Washington, D.C. Valonda returned to North Carolina as a news reporter and anchor for WNCT-TV in Greenville. In Raleigh, Valonda was an anchor and reporter for WRAL-TV. When WNCN launched the lifestyle show My Carolina Today, creators called on Valonda to host. She interviewed and danced with The Rockettes and Cirque Du Soleil and interviewed many stars, including Marlon Wayans, Jayne Seymour, and Anthony Anderson. A dancer and cheerleader since her early years, Valonda cheered in college and the NFL for the Washington Football Team. Whether serving on the PTA, mentoring girls, or giving her time at a local food pantry, Valonda embraces the verse, "to whom much is given, much is required." That philosophy led Valonda to Delta Sigma Theta Sorority Inc., which she joined in 1993. In 2013, Winston-Salem State University named Valonda a 40 under 40 award winner. In 2015, she was inducted into the university's C. E. Gaines Hall of Fame. Currently, Valonda is a spokesperson for University Ford in Durham, a freelance TV host for Fox 50, and a game show host for the North Carolina Lottery. You might also catch Valonda on TV or the web acting in commercials and corporate videos. Valonda is a media trainer at Walk West and a dance teacher at North Carolina Dance Institute in Raleigh. She is a proud wife to Randal and mother to Lilyn.

CONNECT WITH VALONDA ONLINE:

ValondaCalloway.com

Instagram: @ValCalTV

Twitter: @ValCalTV

Facebook: Valonda Calloway On TV

Made in the USA
Columbia, SC
16 February 2021